DIRECT
MAIL

CHARLES MALLORY

KOGAN
PAGE

Acknowledgements

Special thanks go to the direct mail experts who allowed me to use portions of their work for this book: Joan Throckmorton, author of *Winning Direct Response Advertising*; Jack Schmid & Associates; and William Steinhardt of Steinhardt Direct. Also, thanks to Radio Advertising Bureau's *Sound Management* for letting me reproduce a brief article from the publication.

First published in the United States of America, entitled *Direct Mail Magic*, in 1991 by Crisp Publications Inc, 95 First Street,
Los Altos, California 94022, USA.

This edition first published in Great Britain in
1992 by Kogan Page Ltd, 120 Pentonville Road, London N1 9JN.

British Library Cataloguing in Publication Data

A CIP record for this book is available from the British Library.

ISBN 0-7494-0569-4

Typeset by Witwell Ltd., Southport, Merseyside

Printed and bound in Great Britain by Biddles Ltd., Guildford and Kings Lynn

DIRECT
MAIL

◄ CONTENTS ►

Direct mail/direct marketing/mail order – What's the difference? *9*; Why and how does it work? *9*; No competition? *10*; Knowing what people need and want *11*; Checklist: Exactly what do I need to do? *12*; Which elements are the most important? *13*; Timing your mailing *14*; How you can use direct mail *15*; Constructing the offer *16*

How to select and rent a mailing list *18*; Types of list *20*; What to look for in a list *22*; Analysing the list *23*; Other options for finding lists *24*; How do you merge and purge? *25*

Budgeting your direct mail campaign *26*; Testing the list and your offer *27*; Calculating your return on investment *30*; Choosing a format *31*; A response card shortcut *33*; Where do I draw the line? *34*

Putting offer, package and copy together *36*; Writing the copy *39*; Ten-point A-B-C checklist *40*; 14 attention-getting approaches *41*; Get attention through these 20 approaches *44*; A handy thesaurus of verbs for direct mail copy *44*; The most powerful words *46*; The big 96 *47*; Creating the design *48*

Separating your lists for tracking results *49*; Working with a printer *50*; Working with a mailing house *51*; Mailsort *52*

◄ INTRODUCTION ►

When I did my first direct mail project, it was definitely done with a trial-and-error approach. In my job in public relations, I needed direct mail to support some telephone sales efforts. Because I was the departmental manager and worked directly for the managing director, I didn't have a supervisor to show me the way. I relied on many others where I worked, but didn't even know what questions to ask. For instance, it didn't occur to me to think about the thickness of the response card until the Post Office told me the paper used for the response card was too thin. I didn't know I could save money by using Mailsort. I didn't have a budget to cover a direct mail consultant, although soon I wished I had.

I won't embarrass myself by mentioning the many mistakes on my first project. Fortunately, there were no Post Office penalties, and none of the mailing pieces had to be reprinted. Most important, we got results that were good enough to encourage me to continue.

When I started my own firm, I had enough experience to offer direct mail consulting as part of my services. But I'll always remember that first overwhelming project.

When I was doing that project, I went to three local libraries to find an easy-to-use direct mail guide for someone with little or no experience in the field. Though I found many good books about the theory of direct marketing, writing direct marketing copy and similar topics, I never found an all-encompassing, easy-to-use guide. I checked *Books in Print* and found some more books. No easy-to-use guide. So I wrote one.

Charles Mallory

CHAPTER 1

DEVELOP A DIRECT MAIL STRATEGY

Direct mail/direct marketing/mail order – What's the difference?

Direct mail is one element of *direct marketing*. Direct marketing is a way to market products or services outside the retail system. People who sell by telephone are doing direct marketing, but, of course, not direct mail. Direct marketing includes a variety of ways to sell products. TV channels that sell products are using direct marketing, and so are magazine advertisements urging you to join a record club. *Mail order* is simply another name for direct mail.

Direct mail is another name for mail order

Direct mail is certainly not an experimental form of advertising. Its use has doubled in Britain between 1983 and 1989, and the increase in the number of households favours its use even more in the future. Business-to-business mailings have increased by over one-third in the same period.

Why and how does it work?

Direct mail provides a unique opportunity to target your customers, hence the word *direct*. It's true that you can advertise in a magazine that has a readership profile similar to your customer profile; however, even that audience cannot be segmented as accurately as direct mail.

You *choose* which customers to approach

Example An exclusive jewellery shop wants to advertise its

9

Target high-income postcodes if you are selling expensive items

custom-made jewellery. The manager can choose to advertise in the country magazine, which is upmarket and glossy, and which has a reader profile that is close to the shop's customers. It is obvious, however, that not every reader is a potential customer. Many readers do not have the median £50,000 income that is stated in the readership profile. Many may get the magazine just to see what concerts and other events are being held, while other readers only subscribe for 'coffee table' effect and do not go through the whole magazine. And so on.

A better alternative for the jewellery shop owner may be to acquire the mailing list from the magazine, create an attractive mailing piece, and then 'purge' the list of the postcodes of neighbourhoods with lower median incomes. The owner can even target only subscribers who live in the city's high-income postcodes, thus reaching an even higher-income market. Or the shop owner may elect to use both methods to market the jewellery, as each message would tend to reinforce the other.

No competition?

Some direct mail experts say that direct mail has no competition. Newspapers and magazines have many ads on various pages; TV has many sounds and images, all barking for the sale; and radio stations sandwich ad after ad so that they can offer 'a 30-minute music sweep' of songs only. A direct mail piece, individually encased in its envelope, does not present readers with competing messages.

A mail shot that looks like a personal letter becomes 'awaited' mail

This is not the case. Most homes receive several pieces of direct mail every day. More importantly, direct mail is competing with something called *awaited mail*: cheques, letters from friends, ordered merchandise and other items are pulled from the stack first with intense interest. Some people throw direct mail away unopened, but that number is relatively small. Despite the abundance of today's direct mail pieces, people are still concerned about the possibility of throwing away something valuable. Direct mail that is sent first class and/or looks like a personal letter virtually becomes awaited mail, because the recipient wants to know who sent it. This interest may even allow direct mail to outdo awaited mail in reader attention.

Direct mail has the distinct advantage of being a more personal buying experience than most other marketing forms. It is more personal to look at your own four-colour catalogue of clothing in the comfort of your living room than it is to push through crowds at the shopping centre. It is more effective to read about forth-coming seminars while checking your personal organiser than it is to see the listing of seminars offered while glancing at the morning paper in the kitchen when your organiser is on your desk. And filling in the blanks on a response card is usually quicker and less annoying than phoning a number that gives you a message every 30 seconds that says, 'All customer service lines are busy. Please continue holding. Calls will be answered in the order in which they are received.'

Direct mail involves shopping in the comfort of one's own home

Knowing what people need and want

Before you construct your offer, it's a good idea to examine human needs and wants. This will help you to focus on creating an offer that is more likely to be a success.

Your offer should meet people's needs and/or wants

Human needs and wants
According to William Glasser, author of *Control Theory*, human beings have five priority 'needs':

- To survive and reproduce
- To belong
- To have power
- To have freedom
- To have fun.

They also have ten 'wants' (not in order of priority):

- To make and/or save money
- To save time
- To have tasks made easier or eliminated, especially routine ones
- To be comfortable
- To have good health
- To enjoy popularity/praise/style
- To be intelligent
- To gratify curiosity/satisfy appetite
- To possess beautiful or coveted things
- To be individual.

Checklist: Exactly what do I need to do?

You need to start planning early

For many businesses and entrepreneurs, a basic mailing is a good start. (If you need to do a catalogue or multi-part mailing and have no experience, you should work with a direct mail consultant because of the complexity of the job.)

Here's a checklist of the steps for doing a basic direct mailing. Tick each of them as you progress in your project. Look at the whole list before you use it. Depending on your particular circumstances, some of the components might be in slightly different order.

1. ☐ Understand what your customers and prospects want to buy.

2. ☐ Determine whether direct mail is really superior (for your type of business) to other marketing methods – public relations, space advertising and telephone sales, for example – or whether it is at least worth testing.

3. ☐ Review other companies' direct mail pieces, especially those from competitors.

4. ☐ Draft a basic budget.

5. ☐ Construct your offer.

6. ☐ Set a schedule for completion. Set beginning and end dates for these steps:

    (a) Developing the package and creative concept. Allow 2-8 weeks (more if you plan to use outside writers and designers, or if the mailing piece is particularly complicated).
    (b) Acquiring the mailing list. Allow 2-4 weeks.
    (c) Printing the pieces. Allow 1-6 weeks.
    (d) Preparation by the mailing house. Allow 1-4 weeks.
    (e) Mailing date.

7. ☐ Check the current mailing requirements with your Royal Mail account manager.

8. ☐ Determine the package components (formal letter with response card, for example) and Mailsort delivery option.

9. ☐ Determine the number of people to whom you will mail.

10. ☐ Set a detailed budget.

11. ☐ Review possible mailing lists and choose one or more.

12. ☐ Write the copy and create the artwork, or engage copy-writers and designers to do it.

13. ☐ Get printing quotations (based on finished artwork and copy), and get prices from mailing services if needed. Double check the size and weight of your finished piece – *before* it is printed.

14. ☐ Send the camera-ready artwork to the printer; schedule with a mailing house if needed.

15. ☐ Plan a response mechanism procedure (temporary workers to fill orders, salespeople to take telephone enquiries, salespeople who will call on customers, etc).

16. ☐ Send printed pieces to the mailing house. (It might be most efficient to have your printer do this.)

17. ☐ Begin tracking results as responses arrive.

18. ☐ After most responses are in, analyse the mailing and determine which components were successful or weak.

19. ☐ Add all respondents to your own in-house mailing list system.

20. ☐ Rent out your in-house list as soon as it becomes substantial and/or useful enough (a list broker can tell you).

Which elements are the most important?

There is a complex relationship between all the elements of a direct mail piece. The important elements are the lists used, the offer itself, the format of the mailing piece, the effectiveness of the copy, and the timing of the mailing. Based on manipulation of these elements, your response rate may vary as much as:*

The relationship between the elements of a mail shot is important for success

Lists used	1000%
Offer made	300%
Format used	150%
Copy used	50%
Timing of mailing	20% and more

* Information reprinted by permission of J Schmid & Associates Inc, Shawnee Mission, Kansas, USA

Brilliant copy will not sell to the wrong list

Keep in mind that all these elements work together. You can't ignore the timing because you have a fantastic list, even though the two items are very different in how they influence your results. And the most brilliant copy in the world can't sell products to the wrong list.

Items which affect mailing results include:

- A reply-card envelope or card
- A 24-hour phone or fax response number
- Payment by credit card
- An incentive to buy, such as a free gift for orders over a certain value
- Price variation.

Timing your mailing

Good timing of a mail shot is vital for success

Knowing when to mail is very important. It might be based on your particular business. If you're going to send a mailing to announce a special event at your shop, for instance, you might mail a month before the event.

You can devise a strategy for your mailing that will improve your results. According to a leading US direct marketing firm, tests show that some months are more responsive than others in direct mail. The table below shows the relative effectiveness of each month of the year in the USA. (January is the most effective month; February is 96 per cent as effective, and so on.)

100 = Best time to mail	
January	100
February	96
March	71
April	72
May	72
June	67
July	73
August	87
September	79
October	90
November	81
December	79

Keep in mind that this does not preclude common sense. For example, you will not sell many toys at regular prices in January, because of the many reduced-price toy sales in the pre-Christmas season, and demand is reduced in the New Year anyway.

Catalogue mailings are a special case; the best months to mail catalogues are September and October. For business-to-business mailings, January and September are the best months.

How you can use direct mail

Direct mail can be used to accomplish many marketing goals. Tick the objectives that are applicable to your situation:

A checklist of marketing goods for which direct mail is appropriate

☐ To bring new customers into the shop;

☐ To obtain repeat business from current customers:

☐ To identify leads for the field sales force;

☐ To identify leads for telephone sales follow-up;

☐ To do post-sales follow-up;

☐ To announce something new – a product or service, or an upgrade of a product or service;

☐ To support other advertising (TV/radio/newspaper/magazine advertising or public relations).

Think of other goals that would benefit your business:

☐ _____

☐ _____

☐ _____

☐ _____

☐ _____

☐ _____

☐ _____

☐ _____

☐ _____

Constructing the offer

Decide what you want the customer to do

Some basic offers are listed below. Develop an offer that is most suitable for your business. Don't be over-ambitious. If you own a retail business, a free demonstration is a perfectly fine offer. You can also combine offers. For example, you can offer a percentage-off sale for a limited time. This list will get you started with your own ideas; it does not represent all possible kinds of offer.

Sale
● A percentage off
● Time limit
● Seasonal
● Certain items or group of items (all men's clothing, shoes)
● Reason-why sale (overstock, slightly damaged)

Free
● Gift with purchase
● Catalogue
● Amount-off coupon/certificate
● Estimate
● Sample
● Delivery

Guarantee
● Money back
● Multiple amount of money back (double, triple, etc)
● Free trial

You might be planning to use direct mail to invite customers to an open house. Is that an offer? In a sense. You are inviting others to see a new, renovated or changed business. But the invitation can be enhanced by using one of the others listed above.

Examples of direct mail offers

> # Come to our open day – and get a 25% discount on all merchandise!

> # OPEN DAY
> Free 'Managing DOS' booklet just for
> viewing our new line of personal computers!

> # OPEN DAY
> *Sign up for free draws – dinners for two and theatre tickets.*

Remember, it doesn't have to be simple if you don't want it to be. One innovative company started a hosiery club and customers carried membership cards. After each purchase of stockings, the card was punched, and after 12 purchases, the customer received a pair of stockings free. The original mailing piece included a card for all recipients, and the customer got the impression that the card made her a member of an exclusive club.

Successful offers do not have to be simple

Exercise
Write some offer ideas for your business in the space provided below:

_____

_____

_____

_____

_____

_____

_____

_____

_____

_____

_____

_____

◀ CHAPTER 2 ▶

FINALISE YOUR LIST

How to select and rent a mailing list

Buying or renting a list saves time

Unless you have compiled your own mailing list, you will need to buy or rent one for your mailing. It is far more common to *rent* a list than to buy one. It is also far less expensive to rent an already compiled list that represents potential buyers for your product or service than to create your own list from scratch. Your primary goal is to create a profitable return from a direct mailing.

Others have used and probably will use the same list you are renting, but if you've chosen the right list, this will not affect your response rate. Here are the steps to take in renting a list:

How

Using a list broker

Find a list broker. A list broker finds lists and rents them to those who want them. Get recommendations of list brokers from other businesses that have sent direct mail, or check local Yellow Pages under 'Direct Mail'. Trade magazines can also provide names.

If you would like to buy a mailing list for your exclusive use, check with a list broker.

Tip: Do your own research. Evaluate your customers to help you rent the right list, and build up your own

Although list brokers will work with your marketing plan and recommend lists, you should do your own research. Nobody knows your business and your customers better than you do. Develop an approach to evaluate your customers – age, sex, income level, preferences and other psychological and demographic factors. Review the *profile sheets* provided by list brokers. These sheets give information about names on the list in a variety of categories, and will help you to select the lists that are right for your audience and offer.

To get an idea of what lists are available, consult *Lists and Data Sources* (Ladson House), published twice annually.

Cost

Renting a list usually costs between £50 and £200 per thousand names, with additional minor costs for formatting or special sorting. If you are using Mailsort, you need to specify 'Mailsort order' to the list provider as this ensures that labels are provided as required by the mailing house, including gaps between geographical areas in the list.

Calculate the costs of list rental

You do not have to pay a broker's fee; he or she receives a percentage of the rental as commission.

Format

Decide in what form you want your mailing list. Here are three basic formats and how they are used. Tick the one that is most appropriate for you.

Mailing list format

☐ *Mag tape*
A computer tape is used for large-number mailings (1000+) when the address will be imprinted directly on to the printed material, or when you want to personalise a letter *and* print labels.

☐ *Disks*
Microcomputer disks are useful when a mailing will be generated by your computer. Highly suitable when you rent a list for unlimited use rather than for a one-time mailing, but this is costly.

☐ *Labels*
Use labels when you don't need the names and addresses printed on other materials. Labels can be purchased in Cheshire or self-adhesive form – which means that the name/address block is positioned for special machines that cut, paste, and apply them to the mailing piece. Alternatively, they can be purchased in pressure-sensitive form for hand application to envelopes or other printed pieces. Decide whether your labels will be machine-applied or hand-applied.

Lead time

How long does it
take for your
selected list to be
delivered?

Ask your broker how long after you sign the contract it will take to receive your mailing list. Generally, it takes two to three weeks from the time you enquire and sign the contract to when you receive the list, although with special arrangements an order can be rushed.

More details about getting a list

**Facts about using a
rented list**

- Most list owners require a copy of what you will send as a direct mail piece. This is to ensure that the piece is in good taste or that closely competing organisations do not use the same lists. If you can print your piece before you choose the list, you'll be prepared. If not, send a draft of the copy that has been written, along with a rough design of the piece. After your piece is printed, send a sample to the list owner, even if you've already used the list.
- Unless special arrangements are made, lists are rented for one-time use only. Lists are seeded with disguised names so that users who violate this rule will be discovered.
- You do not own a list when you rent it to mail your piece. If someone on the mailing list responds by sending you a card or replies in some way that gives you their name, address, and other information, you now own these names and can use them to compile your own mailing list.

Types of list

There are three types of list: each one has advantages and disadvantages.

Type	Advantages	Disadvantages
1. House list A list of an organisation's own customers.	Strong customer base; proven buyers.	Can be overused by owner; expensive to compile; takes time to build.
Example: List of customers who have purchased major appliances from an electrical store, compiled from response or warranty cards sent back to the store. Response cards contain name, address, customer service information (satisfaction level), and other data.		

Type	Advantage	Disadvantage
2. Response list People who have taken action to be on a list by joining, subscribing, buying, phoning, applying for credit.	Contains names of people who are interested in the product or service and who are more likely to respond to or read related mail; a relatively homogeneous group (likely to have common interests).	Selection of the right list is difficult because of numerous choices; list does not contain proven buyers.

Examples: Subscribers to magazines and newspapers; members of social, political, professional and other organisations; people who have applied for a credit card in the past six months; people who have purchased from a department store catalogue in the past year.

Type	Advantage	Disadvantage
3. Compiled list A universe of names, compiled from other lists or directories.	Good for blanket coverage of an area; less expensive.	Few or no segmentations based on market data; duplicated names can be as high as 5 per cent. More likely to contain wrong addresses.

Examples: Names of all adults living within a given postcode; names compiled from a city directory; names compiled from a telephone directory.

Business-to-business lists

There are also business-to-business lists, which are used by businesses to market directly to specific kinds of other businesses. These can be targeted to particular positions in businesses – for example, to the managing directors in a listing of advertising agencies. Or

Business mailings to other businesses

you could mail to all human resource directors at companies in the pharmaceuticals industry. If this is how your business operates, you'll want to use this type of list.

What to look for in a list

The questions to ask when you are considering list rental

When you review possible lists, look for demographic and other characteristics that will give you a close match to your ideal market. List brokers can provide printed information that answers many of these essential questions. If you do not find a particular bit of information on the list description sheet, ask your broker if he or she can find the information.

Do not be dismayed if you cannot find answers to each and every one of these questions. For some questions, especially the *qualitative* ones, the information might not be available. All the *quantitative* information should be there.

A fictitious profile is given here as an example

Questions to ask	Sample description sheet
1. Name of list?	Current year home buyers in the county of Barsetshire
2. Total number of names?	56,000
3. Cost?	£70/K (£70 per 1000 names)
4. How was list compiled?	From estate agencies' sales reports
5. Date list compiled?	October (previous year)
6. What is the list profile?	
–Age	Average age 36
–Sex	51% male, 49% female
–Income	£24,300 median family income
–Housing	
• Size of unit	Average 1200 square feet
• Length of residence	0 years
• Owner/renter	100% owners
• Home value	Average £85,000
• Age of unit	Average 22 years
• Plot size	Average 3000 square feet
–Buying style	
• Mail order buyer	Not available
• Purchase history	Not available
• Credit history	Available
• Special interests	Not available

Questions to ask	Sample description sheet
–Family life cycle	
• Young singles	1%
• Newly married, no children	12%
• Married with children	81%
• Empty nest	5%
• Solitary survivor	1%

> **Note:** This profile is fictitious and was created for the purposes of this book. It does not present actual data.

Analysing the list

Take a look at the sample description just given (pages 22–3). Let's say we are looking for a list for a mailing to find patients for a county network of dental clinics.

Read between the lines to find out if a list will suit your needs

Many aspects of the list look good. The cost, £70/K, or £70 per thousand, is inexpensive. It is recent enough – it contains home buyers compiled in the past year. If we were planning to use a list to sell carpet cleaning services to people who had just bought carpeting, a more up-to-date figure – such as all people who bought carpeting in the past *three months* – would be needed.

Details of home and plot size and buying style are acceptable and not of major concern. The income level is all right. The length of residence is listed as zero because each buyer added to the list had just bought the home. The people on this list have bought a house within the past year and obviously are not likely to have moved away since they made the purchase; therefore, the accuracy rate should be high.

Since these are new home buyers, the list will include some people who are new to the region in which they bought their home. They are likely to be interested in knowing about a dentist on whom they can rely. And though everybody should go to the dentist, we know that children are a prime market – and 81 per cent of the people on this list have children who live at home.

But *one important factor*: the list was compiled from estate agencies, meaning that *those who rent, already own a home,* or *bought a house directly from the owner* are not included in this list.

Perhaps this is not a problem – or could it mean the omission of thousands of higher-income, bigger-family, more recent names?

After you ask your broker for description sheets from several lists that might suit your needs, take your time in analysing them. This requires reading the information – and then reading between the lines.

Other options for finding lists

Option 1

You can buy lists without going to a broker

You do not have to go to a list broker to get a list. Some business people choose to find the appropriate list through a directory or by recognising a valuable list just from observation.

For instance, if you receive a catalogue containing upmarket women's clothing, and you are selling similar items, you can contact the catalogue company and attempt to rent their list of customers who have purchased from the catalogue.

It is even possible to circumvent the list-broker middleman and obtain a better deal. The most common commission paid to a list broker is 10 to 20 per cent. The commission is paid by the list owner to the broker, and it is standard practice for a list to cost the same whether it is rented from the organisation or through a broker. Why? The organisation accepts lower profit and pays the broker the commission when the list is rented because the broker did the work of finding a list renter.

You may be able to negotiate a discount

Sometimes, if you approach the list owner directly, you can negotiate a discount equivalent to the commission paid to the list broker. Don't assume that you must be given a discount just because you do not use a broker; some organisations adhere to a cost-per-thousand that is non-negotiable.

Option 2

Mailing houses that offer full service mailing will also act as list brokers

Many mailing houses offer full-service mailing. If you plan to use them for other services, such as printing, imprinting addresses, stuffing and sorting, mailing, and other services, they will also gladly serve as list broker. Get to know your account representative at such a company to assess the value of this approach. Make certain that the person working with you in selecting a list is knowledgeable about direct mail lists. Keep in mind that the

24

organisation is acting as a broker, so you will not be able to achieve the discount mentioned in option 1 above.

To eliminate hassles, some businesses are going to full-service mailing houses for the entire programme: generating the idea, copywriting and design, printing, finding a mailing list, and handling all aspects of mailing to the consumer. This might be suitable for you, but you will probably pay a higher rate because services (writing, designing, printing) are often contracted to freelances and then marked up in price by the mailing house.

How do you merge and purge?

A term often used in direct mail is *merge and purge*. This is a computer-run operation used when you mail to more than one list in a single mailing. Two or more lists can be *merged* and then duplicate names are *purged* from the list. If you use a list broker request the combined list be provided this way (there may be an added charge for the service). Purging is also known as de-duplicating.

Join lists together then delete the duplicates

Example: An entrepreneur who has a one-person operation providing career consulting and CV writing decides to do a mailing to three lists:

- Graduates (current year and the past two years) of a local polytechnic – 394 names.
- Subscribers to a named business magazine – 12,400 names.
- Members of the Advertising and Public Relations Club – 692 names. (This is the entrepreneur's experimental list; she knows that job-hopping is more prevalent in these businesses.)

The three lists are merged, then purged. Let's say there are 230 names who are on more than one list. That eliminates 230 pieces of mail, because those 230 will get *one* copy of the piece instead of two or three. Merging and purging the three lists not only saves the entrepreneur a few pounds, but more importantly, the mailing is more effective to those 230 people because they aren't annoyed by getting two or three copies of the same piece.

◀ CHAPTER 3 ▶

TESTING AND BUDGETING

Budgeting your direct mail campaign

Budgeting helps to estimate your probable profitability and whether you are getting an acceptable return on your investment. It is projected further on pages 30–31

First-time direct mailers often make the mistake of not thoroughly budgeting all the costs of a direct mail campaign, and then looking at whether the campaign will be profitable at an acceptable rate. Like any other marketing effort, direct mail must be analysed on the basis of *return on investment* (ROI).

You begin by determining what an appropriate return on investment is for your company. Depending on what kind of business you are in and what your normal ROI is, this can range from as low as 5 per cent to as high as 30 per cent. If you usually get an ROI of 20 per cent in your business, you should get at least that from a direct mail campaign; if your profit projections for a direct mail campaign fall below that, you should probably invest your money in some other marketing effort that can be counted on to return 20 per cent.

Here is a basic list of the costs that you should include in your budget:

Designing the mailing piece
Creative management
Copywriting
Design and production

Mailing costs
Bulk mail permit, if appropriate
Cost per piece to mail second class or Mailsort

Mailing house costs for attaching labels, stuffing envelopes, sorting for the Post Office, and delivering to the Post Office (ie fulfilment)
Business reply permit
Cost per response for using business reply envelopes or cards

Printing costs
Cost of paper, envelopes and other materials
Cost per piece for printing each part of the package
Charges for delivering to mailing house

List costs
Total number of names you will use, times the cost per thousand
Additional charges for special sorts or for self-adhesive labels

Testing costs
Cost for randomly selected names
Cost for test pieces specially printed at low volume
Cost for mailing house to follow test design

Consulting costs
Cost for consulting time to advise on the offer, packaging, list selection, test design and any other elements of the direct mail plan

When your budget is complete and all costs have been identified, you still need to know what your probable profitability is. This cannot be determined without some knowledge of what the rate of return on the mailing piece is likely to be. You must test the list, and perhaps other elements of the direct mail package, in order to determine the rate of return.

Testing the list and your offer

Even when lists appear to have all the right characteristics to bring in a high rate of response, they sometimes fail to do so. Unless a list is very small – less than 2000 – it is important to test it to make sure you will have a rate of return that meets your profitability goals. It is recommended that you test at least 1000 randomly selected names from a list before you rent the whole list. There might be a minimum order quantity from the broker.

Do a test run before your bulk mailing

You may also want to test the offer itself, or the packaging of the offer. Testing elements of a mailing is a very sophisticated process because the elements may interact in unexpected ways, but testing can make the difference between making or losing significant amounts of money. The larger the investment you are making, the more important it is to test the lists and other elements before you start mailing to thousands of people. If you are undertaking a large investment, you should consult a direct mail expert to help you design your testing process.

Here is a simple test design. Suppose you are a direct mail office supply company, and you want to attract new customers with an offer for microcomputer disks. You have two lists that appear appropriate – 18,000 corporate subscribers to an office management journal, and a list of 10,000 corporate buyers. You are hesitating between using one or both of the lists, and you are also considering making your offer two different ways:

- Offer A: 100 disks for the amazing price of 98p each!
- Offer B: Buy three packs of 25 disks for £98, get a fourth pack free!

Notice that the buyer pays the same amount in either case; however, many people are attracted to offers that give them something free, and you want to know whether this approach will give you a better return.

You can actually test both elements – the two offers and the two lists – using only 1000 names. This is done with a test design called *matrix testing*. Here's how it works. You would create two test pieces, one making Offer A and one making Offer B. Print 500 copies of each piece. Order 500 randomly selected names from each list. The response cards are coded in some way so that you will be able to tell which mailing list each respondent was on. The 1000 pieces are then mailed as shown in the matrix below:

	Offer A	Offer B
List A	250 names	250 names
List B	250 names	250 names

As the responses come in, they are tallied in these four categories, then the rows and columns are added together. Suppose the responses look like this:

	Offer A	Offer B	TOTAL
List A	2 (.8%)	5 (2.0%)	7 (1.4%)
List B	3 (1.2%)	7 (2.8%)	10 (2.0%)
TOTAL	5 (1.0%)	12 (2.4%)	

Your suspicion that people prefer an offer of something free is confirmed; you decide to use Offer B. You should probably use List B for certain, and whether or not you use List A depends on what you learn when you work on your budget and ROI.

A matrix test allows you to get more information from just a few names. More than two elements can be tested in a more elaborate matrix – but you need an expert to design such a test.

Although such a test does not predict with complete precision what your final return will be, it is close enough for you to construct your projected return on investment with confidence.

Getting an early prediction of response rate

If you are on a tight schedule – or just dying to know whether your test shows that your offer and lists were successful – you can cut down on the time needed to predict your response rate by using the principle of the bell curve. The number of responses received in the mail or on the phone, like test scores, tend to fall into a bell-shaped curve. For example, here is a vastly oversimplified example of a response per day count on a mailing of 1000, beginning with the day the first response was received:

Plot your responses on a graph to predict results

		Cumulative responses
Day 1	1	1
Day 2	0	1
Day 3	2	3
Day 4	4	7
Day 5	6	13
Day 6	5	18
Day 7	3	21
Day 8	2	23
Day 9	0	23
Day 10	0	23
Day 11	1	24

If you plotted this on a graph, it would look like this:

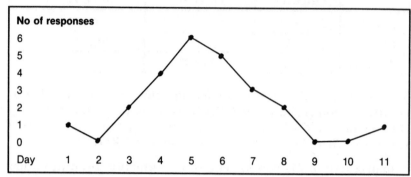

You can see that there is a more or less halfway point at which the number of responses begins to decline. You can use this point to predict the final rate of response. For example, you notice that at day 6, the rate begins to decline, and you guess that 50 per cent of the responses are now in, or rather that they were in by day 5. If the final count is twice the cumulative count for day 5, 26 responses will be received, for a response rate of 2.6 per cent. This is not a completely accurate predictor – in our example, the final count was 24, for a 2.4 per cent response rate. But it is an indicator that can be useful – at least you know the rate is very unlikely to be below 1 per cent or over 3 per cent. As you get more experience of doing tests in your market, you will be able to predict from the curve with increasing accuracy.

Calculating your return on investment

These calculations are essential if you are to be profitable

With a detailed budget and a proposed return rate, you are ready to project your probable ROI. This is a perfect exercise for a spread-sheet program on a computer. Spreadsheets make it easy to ask 'What if . . .?' types of question . . . so that you can immediately see the effect of changing some element of the package. For example, if your projection is disappointing, you might see whether the ROI becomes satisfactory if you decide to have respondents use their own stamps rather than your paying the postal charges for a prepaid response card. You would need to adjust your response rate downward since people are somewhat more likely to respond if they don't have to provide a stamp.

Let's continue the example of the disks offer. You decide to use only List B. Your test indicates a rate of return between 2.8 per cent (Offer B, List B) and 2.4 per cent (all Offer B). Here is a typical ROI analysis:

Direct mail costs

	£
Number to be mailed: 10,000	
Cost per piece (printing, materials)	0.57
Mailing costs per piece (postage, mailing house)	0.42
Cost of list (£75/M, or /0.75 each)	0.075
TOTAL COST PER PIECE	£1.065
Cost per piece x 10,000	£10,650
One-time costs (postal permits, creative services, testing, consulting)	£9,450
TOTAL COSTS	£20,100

Projected income

Average order amount £100

Income at 2.4% return £24,000	(240x100)
Income at 2.8% return £28,000	(280x100)

Return on investment

At 2.4% £24,000–£20,100	equals £3,900
ROI 19.40%	(£3,900÷20,100)
At 2.8% £28,000–£20,100	equals £7,900
ROI 39.30%	(£7,900÷20,100)

If your business should get at least a 20 per cent ROI, this shows you need to trim your expenses a fraction.

It is better to cancel a campaign after a test that indicates that the concept will not work. Many inexperienced direct-mailers do not do the essential testing, budgeting and ROI projections. If a campaign is not well constructed, you can actually lose more money with every additional piece you mail – not a good way to do business!

Cancel a campaign if the projections indicate you will lose money

Choosing a format

A wide variety of formats is possible. Just take a look at some of the direct mail offers you've received and you'll see what I mean. There are black-and-white pieces printed on inexpensive paper, and expensive, four-colour, glossy pieces; there are simple letter-in-

Choose a simple package to start with, using standard sized paper and envelope

31

envelope pieces and fold-out brochures. There are many options for packaging your offer.

A simple package might be a good idea if this is your first venture in direct mail. Remember, though, that the main criterion is the piece's ability to produce results. A hairstyling salon that wants to attract customers by announcing that they've just hired a new, popular stylist could simply send an attractive four-colour postcard with the news; that might be all the 'package' that is needed. A basic package might include a letter, some mechanism for a response and, if necessary, a brochure.

Letter
The letter introduces your product or service to the recipient, and can be printed on letterhead, special stationery just for this mailing, or plain paper.

Outer envelope
This will contain all the pieces; a blurb can be printed on the outside, and a return address might also be on the envelope.

Response mechanism
This can be a tear-off portion of the letter (perhaps perforated by the printer), a separate card, or other device.

Brochure
Although a brochure is not essential, many direct mail shots contain some piece to accompany the letter. It more fully describes and demonstrates your product or service.

Business reply envelope
If your response mechanism is not a business reply card (which is self-mailing), a business reply envelope further pushes the recipient to answer.

Use enticing copy that encourages the recipient to act *now*

Sometimes it's *how* you treat the particular piece that determines the format. A basic package can be hard-sell, containing an outer envelope filled with blurbs ('YOU might be the next big winner in the Super Sweepstakes!') with busy, wealth-promising artwork on the inner pieces. You can use a *lift letter,* which is often seen in magazine-subscription approaches that have a 'Yes, I'll subscribe' envelope and a 'No' envelope. Sticking out of the 'No' envelope is a lift letter that says, 'Please don't say no – not now!'

A mailing piece can be highly personalised, especially when laser printing is used. Sometimes a piece is printed with a line left blank; then that line is lasered in. That's why some sweepstake pieces look like this:

> Just imagine, MR JONES . . . all your friends in ELM STREET will envy you as you cruise down the street
> *in your new car!*

A good rule of thumb is that the fancier a package is, the more it costs. Determine what product or service your customers and prospects want to buy and how that mailing piece should sell to them. This is common sense. If you own a shop that sells gourmet cooking items and has classes in gourmet cooking, the potential customers need to see mouth-watering colour photos of food; hard-sell copy in black-and-white is the wrong approach. Or another example: if you're mailing to your own list of previous customers, don't waste your money with lasered-in names and addresses to personalise the letter.

A response card shortcut

To increase effectiveness and accuracy in your mailings, it's a good idea to use a label or mag tape address on the response card or form itself. This address can be coded to identify instantly which list the name was on, which helps you to track your results accurately. This technique also reduces the amount of time needed for your customer or prospect to fill in an order form, since the name and address are already there.

Computerised lists enable you to code responses

Example 1

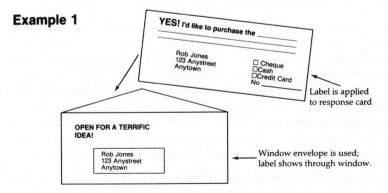

Label is applied to response card

Window envelope is used; label shows through window.

Example 2

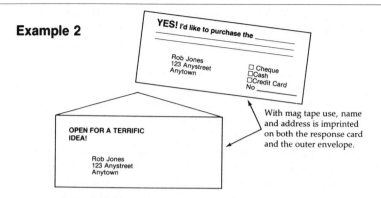

With mag tape use, name and address is imprinted on both the response card and the outer envelope.

Where do I draw the line?

A 'quality' mailing tends to attract a better response

It's confusing to work out how expensively or cheaply to produce a direct mail piece. You would think that top quality paper, an expensive, well-designed envelope, and copy written by an expensive professional would always do better than an inexpensive mailing that you and your own staff might create. The assumptions do not always hold true. Sometimes an expensive direct mail piece is less effective than a more cheaply produced one.

Generally, a heavier, costlier letterhead gives a better impression and may create more responses than inexpensive paper; a four-colour brochure usually draws more responses than a two-colour brochure. Even when these rules of thumb are true in some markets, they may not work in yours. Some of the most profitable pieces ever used are design horrors – busy and inelegant. You can test each design, of course, but this is expensive. Common sense and market knowledge make a big difference.

Your goal is to create the highest response possible within your budget. When making your plans, strike a balance between economical and luxurious, unless your product or service strictly calls for one or the other. A classy jewellery shop needs an expensive package to create an appropriate image; a non-profit community organisation might not want to have a package that is too slick – it might make contributors think they're giving donations to the organisation's printer! Some non-profit organisations get their direct mail materials donated and state this on the package.

Direct mail is the business of testing. Here's a rule to live by that will help you to know when to draw the line:

Rule 1, 2, 3 to infinity
Keep accurate and detailed records of your direct mail programmes including all elements and costs, a copy of the complete package, final rates of return and ROI. Learn what works and what doesn't for your organisation. Once you have the numbers, analyse them to plan your next move.

Keep careful records of your mailings and analyse the results for future use

CHAPTER 4

DEVELOP YOUR CREATIVE APPROACH

Putting offer, package and copy together

Plan your mailing package

Once you've determined what your offer will be and how you will package it, it's time to write the copy. Even if you engage a writer, suggest that he or she use the creative strategy outline shown in the example below. This is the genesis of the copy and graphic design that will shape the final direct mail piece. The creative strategy outline was created by Joan Throckmorton.

Creative Strategy Outline	
Title of Job:	*Vital Woman* magazine, the first comprehensive magazine devoted to women's health and fitness.
Competition:	None. This is the first such publication.
Market:	Active, busy women between the ages of 18 and 34. (Women who have shown an interest in health and fitness publications, exercise book buyers, etc.)
Offer:	Charter offer, 1 year for £15; full money-back guarantee. Premium ('Answers to 24 of Women's Most Troublesome Health Questions').

Hypothesis:	Women want to be better informed about their health and general well-being so they can take control of their lives, make wiser decisions, and improve their relationships with their doctors. This enables them to avoid risk and worry because they can understand and solve or prevent many problems and live a more healthy life.
Copy/Platform Benefits:	*Vital Woman*, the first magazine devoted to women's health and fitness, will enable you to take more responsibility for your own health —via expert medical advice on health and fitness. —via a better understanding of women's health and fitness problems. —via a natural approach to health. The result will be —a better relationship with your doctor. —a healthier, happier life.
First Copy Statement:	You are the primary diagnostician. Let *Vital Woman* help to make sure that the *one* person who can take care of you best does a good job. —Take charge of your own health with *Vital Woman.* —Put your health in the best hands – your own. —Don't waste time and money on unnecessary doctor's visits
Second Copy Statement:	Make sure your doctor takes you seriously. (Why should you feel neurotic every time you feel sick?)
Third Copy Statement:	Attend your local surgery's 'Well Women's Clinic'. Sit down and listen. Ask questions.
Secondary Benefits/ Features:	—Sound information on natural healing (keep medicine and drugs to a minimum) —Pros and cons of major women's health issues

—Reader Qs and As
—Medically approved diets and exercise
—Emotional and interpersonal advice
—10 pages of colour, many illustrations in every issue
—Use deadline for offer
—List full advisory board on first page of letter
—Make the spokesperson a credible woman (female publisher).

·Format: Direct mail package/Second-class mail
Outer envelope
4-page letter (2-colour)
Brochure (4-colour)
Order card
1-page lift letter

Now that you've seen an example, draw up your own creative strategy outline.

Creative strategy outline

Title of Job: _____

_____

Competition: _____

_____

Market: _____

_____

Offer: _____

_____

Hypothesis: _____

_____

Copy Platform/Benefits: _____

_____

First Copy Statement: _____

_____

Second Copy Statement: _____

_____

Third Copy Statement: _____

_____

Secondary Benefits/Features: _____

_____

Recommendations: _____

_____

Format: _____

_____

Reprinted with permission from *Winning Direct Response Advertising* by Joan Throckmorton, Prentice Hall, 1986.

Writing the copy

After developing your creative strategy outline, move on to actually writing the piece. Keep in mind the copy statements you wrote in your creative strategy. Don't create in a vacuum. Allow others, particularly expert friends and colleagues, to review your direct mail copy.

If you're using a freelance writer, feel free to suggest that he or she use this outline approach. It's a good idea to find a freelance copywriter who has previously written direct mail pieces. The stars in the business are somewhat expensive for small businesses, but there are many others who are very good and affordable.

There are ways to find freelance direct mail copywriters if you don't have contacts through business associates:

- Contact the British Direct Marketing Association (BDMA).
- Check the Yellow Pages under Advertising and Direct Mail.
- Read the classified ads in the direct marketing trade press.

Talk to candidates about their previous experience and what pieces they wrote that worked well. Review each writer's portfolio. The sections that follow are useful if you write the copy yourself.

Ten-point A-B-C checklist

Here's an automatic outline you can use when you create your direct mail copy. By placing these proven elements in your direct mail piece, you greatly increase your chance for success. (Useful words and examples follow this checklist.)

Checklist for dynamic direct mail copy

1. ATTAIN ATTENTION	**6. FEATURE SPECIAL DETAILS**
2. BANG OUT BENEFITS	**7. GILD WITH VALUES**
3. CREATE VERBAL PICTURES	**8. HONOUR CLAIMS WITH NO QUIBBLE MONEY-BACK GUARANTEES (SATISFACTION)**
4. DESCRIBE SUCCESS INCIDENT	**9. INJECT ACTION IN READER**
5. ENDORSE WITH TESTIMONIALS	**10. JELL WITH POSTSCRIPT**

Reprinted with permission of William Steinhardt, Steinhardt Direct, Shawnee Mission, Kansas, USA.

14 Attention-getting approaches

Start your direct mail copy by grabbing the reader. It is difficult to get the reader to open the mail; make sure the reader picks up the mailing piece and reads through it. Here are several useful approaches:

Approach	Sample	When to use
1. Invite	I'd like to invite you to sit down with one of the world's greatest books.	To sell a high-resistance item or to sell to a high-resistance audience (for example, people with £50,000 income, who are likely to be busy achievers).
2. Quote	'The great mystery of time, were there no other; the illimitable, silent, never-resting thing called time, rolling, rushing on, swift, silent, like an all-embracing tide.' —Thomas Carlyle.	To evoke emotion; to establish environment; to announce or to say something with authority.
3. Give testimonial	'Our sales increased 15 per cent after we heard his motivating speech!' —Samuel Woodson, director of marketing	To sell a high-resistance item (ie. dating service or time-share apartment); to sell an expensive product or service; to reassure recipient.

Approach	Sample	When to use
4. Identify with	You know how it is at 6pm – everybody's rushing home from work, the kids demand attention, it's time to get dinner . . .	To provoke agreement and gain feeling from recipient that product or service was designed for him or her.
5. Ask 'What if?'	What if your boss called you into his or her office and demoted you – simply because you weren't organised?	To lay groundwork for information to come; to induce recipient to apply the idea to himself or herself and thereby increase your chances for a sale.
6. Question	Do you want to save money every time at the dry cleaners – and on every item?	To get recipient to agree mentally and thereby increase your chances of a sale.
7. State a problem and solution	The air pollution hovering over our city increases 3 per cent per year . . . but you can reverse that trend by joining Clear Air Advocates!	To incite action; to create an environment of group action.
8. Fantasy	Imagine you and your husband sunning yourselves on the beach at St Martinique . . . drinking cool, exotic drinks as you lie on the white sand, the breezes softly caressing your hair . . .	To sell a pricey product or service; to sell a leisure-time item.

Approach	Sample	When to use
9. Tell a story	I announced it: 'I'm going to be a famous pianist.' They all burst into laughter. I'll show them, I thought.	To sell personal improvement.
10. Command	You *cannot ignore* the legislation that your MP is about to introduce.	When the direct mail message is news; when political or social action is sought; to gain interest for a highly competitive product or service (selling cars, for example).
11. Offer a first	You are among the first few people in the nation to receive this special offer.	When it is true and important.
12. Number the ways	You get four great things when you shop at Food Circus: 1. Low prices 2. Friendly service 3. Super Saver Stamps 4. A chance to win a Jetomatic speedboat!	For highly competitive businesses; to persuade customers who are loyal to a competitor.
13. Invoke sympathy	Hungry children cry out in the night . . . you can help with relief through the Concerned and Caring Foster Parents Fund.	To get a response from people who will receive an emotional, rather than tangible, benefit.

Approach	Sample	When to use
14. Use humour	'Knock, knock.' 'Who's there?' 'The present Tsar.' 'The present Tsar who?' 'The present Tsar nice, but the cash is better!'	When selling a light-hearted product or service; to establish a friendly company reputation.

Get attention through these 20 approaches

1. Analogy
2. Quote from *The Oxford* Dictionary of Quotations
3. Command
4. Develop a paradox
5. Exclusive
6. Fantasy
7. Generic
8. Humour
9. Invitational
10. Juxtapose if/assumptive
11. Kindle amusement
12. Laud a hero
13. Manage identification
14. Numbered ways
15. Offer a first
16. Problem/solution
17. Question
18. Relate a story
19. Satire
20. Testimonial

Used with kind permission of William Steinhardt, Steinhardt Direct, Shawnee Mission, Kansas, USA.

A handy thesaurus of verbs for direct mail copy

This list will save your time. It gathers together the most useful verbs for selling copy

When you write direct mail copy, you should repeat your primary message in several different ways. The intent is to sell your product or service effectively. But it is often time-consuming and frustrating to continually try to think of new words.

Some word processing programs have built-in thesauruses, which come in handy for writing copy. Rather than electronically thumbing through lists of words, however, you can always use the following handy guide for finding strong verbs that are useful in writing direct mail copy.

These are grouped into general categories for easy use. They are not listed in order of importance.

Perceive

analyse	evaluate	pinpoint	see
anticipate	identify	rank	spot
assess	know	rate	understand
define	learn	read	
determine	map	recognise	
discern	measure	review	

Strong action

act	deliver	motivate	spend
affect	demand	negotiate	spotlight
assert	direct	praise	stop
boost	empower	promote	streamline
build	express	pull	supervise
charge	frame	reduce	tackle
command	grow	sharpen	take charge
confront	harness	show	thrive
conquer	issue	single out	win
control	leverage	soothe	
defeat	master	speed up	

Organise

concentrate	maximise	plan	select
differentiate	move	prioritise	
garner	organise	save	

Facilitate

accommodate	counsel	inform	remain
acquire	deal with	involve	satisfy
answer	depend	join	segment
apply	develop	keep	situate
approach	devote	learn	sort
balance	ensure	maintain	stick to
bridge	facilitate	manage	sustain
claim	freshen	polish	tap
coach	get	prepare	test
communicate	handle	present	turn
conduct	implement	redirect	use

Achieve

accept	discover	increase	reduce
accomplish	double	influence	resolve
be	establish	make	sell
convert	fit	multiply	shape
create	gain	persuade	strengthen
demonstrate	improve	reach	triple

'Negative' action

avoid	change	lose	sidestep
break	end	overcome	
cancel	intercept	regain	

The most powerful words

When writing your direct mail copy, why not include the most powerful words in the English language, namely:

New   Human beings continually crave novelty.

Save   Everyone wants to save time, energy or money.

Free   Everyone wants something for nothing.

Safety   This word indicates long-lasting product quality and relates to personal security.

Proven   Documentation works. People like to be persuaded.

Love   This word connotes deep inner satisfaction.

Discover   This word stimulates feelings of adventure and excitement.

Guarantee It's what today's consumers demand.

Health   This 'new' consciousness will be with us for a long time.

Results   People want to know what will happen, not what it takes to get there.

You   This is possibly the most important word of all.

Reprinted with permission, Radio Advertising Bureau's *Sound Management*, 304 Park Avenue South, New York, NY 10010, USA.

The big 96

Here are 96 words commonly found in direct mail copy. Writing direct mail copy isn't like fiction, where originality is valued. In direct mail copy, it is a good idea to use popular words because they are proven sellers. They are listed in alphabetical order.

Actual	Accept	Affect	All
Beautiful	Because	Best	Better
Big	Booklet	Comfortable	Complete
Customer	Deep	Discount	Discover
Dozen	Earn	Easy	Endorsed
Extra	Fast	Fine	Free
Future	Full	Genuine	Get
Gift	Give	Good	Great
Guarantee	Handy	Happy	Heavy
High	Home	Idea	Image
Income	Job	Join	Joy
Keen	Keep	Live	Long
Love	Magic	Many	Men
Model	Natural	Need	News
Offer	Original	Personal	Plan
Practical	Protect	Quality	Real
Receive	Reliable	Sample	Satisfaction
Save	Secret	Send	Smooth
Special	Strong	Sure	Surprising
Take	Thousands	Time	Today
Trial	Under	Unit	Update
Useful	Valid	Value	Vary
Venture	Women	Write	X-Ray
You	Yours	Zero	Zip

Used with kind permission of William Steinhardt, Steinhardt Direct, Shawnee Mission, Kansas, USA.

Creating the design

If you're not a designer, don't try to do your own artwork and layout unless it's an extremely simple piece. Find a designer who has done some type of direct mail artwork and, of course, examine his or her portfolio.

A designer should provide sketches or a mock-up of your piece before beginning production and preparing it for printing. Insist on this intermediary step; it is much cheaper to reject a design before rather than after production.

Like the copy, the design should fit what you're doing. Here are some ways for you to determine the appropriateness of the design, whether or not you are experienced in art.

Ask yourself if it fits the following elements:

- The type of business
- The type of product or service offered
- The copy
- The price of the product/service offered.

Here are some other elements to review in the artwork:

- Does the mood of the piece seem right?
- Does it get attention?
- In a brochure, is there a single focus?
- Is the type appropriate for the artwork and the message?
- Is the type large enough to read? (Many people read direct mail very rapidly, and if they have difficulty reading some parts, they pass them by.)

Where do you find designers, if you don't have recommendations from business associates?

- Contact the British Direct Marketing Association.
- Check the Yellow Pages under Advertising, Direct Mail, Artists – Commercial or Designers – Advertising and Graphic.
- Check the *Direct Mail Databook* (Gower).

◀ CHAPTER 5 ▶

PUT IT ALL TOGETHER

Separating your lists for tracking results

If you're mailing from more than one list in a single mailing, track returns for each specific list. Let's go back to that earlier example of the entrepreneur in the career consulting business.

Example: The entrepreneur (career consultant/CV writer) has mailed to three lists:

- Graduates (current year and the past two years) of a local polytechnic – 394 names
- Subscribers to a local business magazine – 12,400 names
- Members of the Advertising and Public Relations Club – 692 names.

The entrepreneur hand-applied these labels, since the list is small. A label from the first list (graduates) appears like this:

```
                              A
Ms Susan E Jones
1234 Anystreet Way
```

Because the second list had 12,400 names, she sent this batch to the mailing service. A label from the second list (subscribers) appears like this:

```
          MAILSORT
Charles Jones
4321·Anystreet Place
```

The third list (club members) had labels that were hand-applied; they looked like this:

```
Bob Wilson         B
1221 Anystreet Lane
```

Our entrepreneur used a response card that had the label on it, mailed in a window envelope. When the results come back, she can identify the first list by the A code in the corner; the third list will have the B code. The list of subscribers was sorted and mailed by first class Mailsort.

Working with a printer

Build up good relationships with your printers. They can be a useful source of advice and support

Except for very small mailings, you will need a printer to print your mailing pieces. Small mailings – 500 or below – can be created on your laser printer, if you have one, but even this might not be the least expensive way to do it.

Here are two tips that will make working with commercial printers more successful:

1. Do not save time on the project by forcing the printer into a rushed deadline. Everybody does this. Plan ahead, put your project into the regular production schedule, and you'll get better results with fewer errors. It doesn't matter that you're the customer – by giving the printer respect and time to print the piece properly, your project will get better treatment.

2. Work with a printer who has produced mailing pieces in the past. These printers understand that they can't substitute a lighter-weight paper at the last minute; or they might recognise that you or your designer have created a piece that violates postal regulations. (The cardinal rule is to *always* check with the Post Office before printing.)

Get three or more printers to quote, based on your artwork. If you don't have specific needs for paper types, ask the printer what is 'on the floor' – sometimes printers have an overstock of paper from other jobs and you can get it at a lower price. See and feel the paper when you do this, so you'll know what you're getting.

Remember that you don't have to go to one printer for everything. If you're mailing a four-colour brochure with a black-and-white letter, you can have the brochure done at one printer, and the letter at another: printers give the best prices for their specialities and this can save significant sums.

If you haven't picked a particular type of paper or are unfamiliar with what's available, a printer might try to 'sell up' by persuading you to go for a paper that must be specially ordered, has a slick, glossy look, or other expensive alternative. Listen, because he or she might be right. But keep your customers and prospects in mind. You created your package with them in mind and built the project around it. Don't change to enamel (slick) paper when you've designed a simple package.

Do not let the printer and mailing house get at odds with each other. Sometimes a mailing house will receive a printed piece and tell you that the printer did such-and-such wrong and it's going to cost more to imprint the addresses. Choose a mailing house *and* printer before you actually start the work with either. Then, if difficulties arise, you can call back and forth to each as the project progresses.

Working with a mailing house

Mailing services will be required if you need letters stuffed, envelopes sealed, postage applied, and other mechanical aspects of actually getting the printed pieces out. Your best lead is to get recommendations from business associates for mailing houses. If that doesn't turn up anything, check the Yellow Pages under Direct Mail.

The mailing house works with you and the printer to get the mail shot into the post

Determine in advance exactly what needs to be done. Here are some likely choices:

- Envelope-addressing (mag tape or laser) or labelling (by machine or hand)
- Inside-addressing (to personalise a letter, response card or other piece)
- Folding (letters, brochures and other applicable pieces)
- Inserting (putting letter, brochure, response card, etc into envelope)
- Sealing envelopes
- Applying postage (stamps by machine or metered)
- Bundling and bagging the mailing pieces
- Delivering the mail to the Post Office.

In short, the mailing house does everything that needs to be done to get the pieces in the mail once the printer has printed them.

Your pieces should not have to be sorted by postcode. You can acquire the mailing list already arranged that way and whether the mailing house is applying labels or using a mag tape, it's their responsibility to keep it in that order.

Tell the mailing house that you will be available while the project is under way and that you are to be alerted if anything unusual turns up. This prevents a mailing house from telling you, after the work is complete, that 'the adhesive on the labels wasn't working and they couldn't be applied by machine, so we had to hand-apply them'. Unfortunately, such situations can occur, and you are then supposed to pay higher than the estimated price.

It's best to get a guaranteed quote on the project. This can be done if you have decided on the specifics of number of pieces and work to be done.

Just after you've selected your printer and before you give the printer your artwork, select your mailing house and then tell your contact at the mailing house who your printer is. Then ask, 'Is there anything the printer should know before they start the work?'

It's likely the answer is 'No.' But it might be, 'Yes, tell them we can't label such-and-such a paper very well on our machines,' or some other important specification.

Mailsort

Direct mail service from Royal Mail

Mailsort is an option available from the Royal Mail to cut postage costs and increase efficiency, and has over 4000 users throughout the UK. Large discounts are available on postage costs and there are several ways in which to increase the efficiency of mailing operations with back-up and support available from the Royal Mail.

There is a range of services available under the Mailsort umbrella for large volume mailings. If an organisation sends out letters, statements, invoices, direct mail, newsletters or catalogues on a regular basis, substantial postage discount can be gained using this system.

To qualify, addresses must be sorted by postcode, and post must consist of a minimum of 4000 letters or 1000 packets at one time. Savings can be anything from 8 to 32 per cent off the standard public tariff. The size of the discount is dependent on the size of the mailing and the amount of sorting done. In addition, the 'straight line pricing' system means that payment is made only for what is actually posted per programme and no more.

Sorting can be done on a computer which involves sorting mail at the addressing stage, using the Mailsort database. (This database can be supplied free of charge from the Royal Mail who can give advice on how to implement it.) Alternatively, mail can be sorted manually and the Royal Mail can suggest efficient procedures and give advice.

Mailsort offers three different delivery options:

- *Mailsort 1* is the service that targets next day delivery for urgent mail.
- *Mailsort 2* targets delivery within three working days and is suitable for routine statements, invoices etc.
- *Mailsort 3* targets delivery within seven working days and is cost-effective for less time-critical mail.

All three delivery options use the same sortation plan so it is possible to switch from one to another without having to change systems.

For publishers, or organisations that produce regular journals, magazines, newsletters etc, the special 'sister service' to Mailsort is called Presstream and offers a variety of benefits and low rates. Presstream uses the same sortation plan as Mailsort, and offers a choice of two different delivery options:

Presstream is the bulk mail service for publishers

- *Presstream 1* targets next day delivery for periodicals published and posted weekly or more frequently.
- *Presstream 2* aims for delivery within three working days for periodicals published and posted at least twice a year.

The Presstream services offer significant savings on the public tariff.

CHAPTER 6

RESULTS THAT MAKE THE DIFFERENCE

How to compile your own list

Once you have compiled it, your own list will be more reliable than those you buy in

Perhaps you haven't yet created a mailing list of your current customers or prospects. Begin doing so immediately. Here are other ways to develop a list. Tick Yes or No to indicate whether these sources are useful to you.

Yes	No	Source
_____	_____	Sign-up sheet in your shop
_____	_____	Members of professional organisations
_____	_____	Members of service organisations
_____	_____	Names from your sales staff
_____	_____	Newspaper listings – births, marriages, engagements
_____	_____	Newspaper listings – job promotions or awards
_____	_____	Telephone directories and city directories
_____	_____	Permits (building, development, repairs, etc)

Think up a few of your own:

_____

_____

_____

_____

It might be tedious, but a few names here and a few names there, and it adds up. You may also have a valuable item to rent – your own mailing list.

But should I?
It seems natural to question renting out your in-house list. After all, it's one of your most valuable resources. However, you might as well, because the names on your list are already on other lists in various ways, and other people are making money on those lists.

You don't have to rent your list to competitors, although in many industries this is common. On a local or regional basis, it might not be wise.

Be sure to 'seed' your list before you do rent it. Add several decoy names and some real but undetectable addresses so you can check unauthorised use. You could use a Post Office box or your home address. You can use a secretary's name and fictitious company name with your own company address (if it isn't instantly recognisable as your business address). Change these decoys periodically.

Your goldmine list
Don't create your own list just to rent it out. Offer new products and services to your in-house mailing list on a regular basis. That's the best direct mail programme you'll find.

Measuring your results

Once your mailing has been done and you've handled the results (hosting your open house, having salespeople follow up the leads, etc), don't assume the project is over. It's time to assess the results of the mailing. This is the only way to ensure that your direct mail programmes get more and more efficient.

How do you compare the cost of a mailing programme to 5000

Renting out your in-house list can provide a valuable source of income. However, insist on seeing the renter's mailing shot – possibly in draft – in case it offers goods or services in direct competition with your own

Constant use of your own list keeps it up to date and highlights 'gone-aways'

people with a piece that was mailed to 40,000? Also, isn't it comparing apples and oranges to measure a four-colour piece against a black-and-white one? Not really. One standard equation you can use to measure your results is:

Promotion Costs ÷ Number of Responses = Cost Per Response
(CPR)

The other standard figure is:

$$\frac{\text{Revenue}}{\text{Promotion Costs}}$$

$\frac{1}{1}$ = same revenue as cost

$\frac{1}{2}$ = revenue was twice the cost

= return rate

Build up a timetable for your direct mail shots and build them into your forward planning

If you have one highly successful mailing and have the budget to try again, do so. Many businesses have learned that direct mail works like science. The response you receive from a list predictably returns similar results during future mailings. Review the steps as listed in this book, and constantly network for tips from other business associates who use direct mail.

How often do I mail in the future?

If you've decided that direct mail is a regular part of your business, you might wonder how often to mail. Because businesses and products are so different, you will need to experiment to learn what works best for you. Following are some options for you to consider. You might do:

- A periodic mailing (every month or six weeks) with a different offer each time;
- Four mailings a year, tied to the specific seasons;
- Frequent mailings in the season in which you need the most business. (This is where timing is important.)
- Staggered mailings to various lists. This is particularly handy if salespeople must personally handle each response

card by calling on the customer. An example would be acquiring a list of 10,000 and then mailing 2000 pieces per time, with each mailing two weeks apart.

Write your own ideas:

● _____

_____

_____

● _____

_____

_____

● _____

_____

_____

● _____

_____

_____

Go for it!

Once you've measured your results and demonstrated that direct mail can improve your business and your profitability, you may wonder how you got along without it. May direct mail work so well for you that it's like magic!

◀ APPENDIX 1 ▶

LEGAL REQUIREMENTS

The Trade Descriptions Act 1968

The Trade Descriptions Act makes it a criminal offence to apply a false trade description to goods or to make false or misleading claims, verbally or in writing, about any goods or services you are offering. This is important to bear in mind when preparing advertisements, mail shots and catalogues.

A false trade description covers statements relating to quantity, size, methods or the place of manufacture, production, processing or reconditioning, composition, fitness for the purpose, strength, performance, behaviour, accuracy and other physical character-istics, testing, approval by any person, previous ownership and any other history.

Misleading bargain offers are also prohibited. A code of practice on pricing is available from HMSO (reference S188/2078).

The British Code of Advertising Practice

Various restrictions apply to goods and services that may be offered and the claims that are made for them. It is particularly important for businesses making offers by direct mail to ensure that their printed matter does not contravene the law. Sensitive subjects include:

- Alcoholic drinks
- Cigarettes and tobacco
- Collectibles

- Cosmetics
- Financial services
- Food
- Hair and scalp products
- Medicinal products and products claiming health-giving qualities
- Offers of employment
- Slimming products
- Vitamins and minerals.

The use of the Code is monitored by the Advertising Standards Authority, and a copy can be obtained from them at 2–6 Torrington Place, London WC1E 7HN; 071-580 5555.

The Committee of Advertising Practice at the same address publishes a leaflet, 'Rules for Direct Marketing including List & Database Management', which initiative is monitored by the Advertising Standards Authority. It provides a self-regulatory framework for direct marketing companies, and to fund it a levy will be imposed on Mailsort postage costs from 6 January 1992.

The Data Protection Act 1984

This Act has the object of protecting individuals from unauthorised use of personal data about them, for instance by computer bureaux selling mailing lists to direct sales organisations. Data users who store personal data relating to other people on a computer system need to register. They have to disclose to the Registrar of Data Protection what lists they hold, how and where they obtained the details on them and for what purposes they intend to use them. They must also undertake not to disclose them to any unspecified third party, or to use them for any purposes other than the declared ones. However, data used for internal administrative purposes, such as payrolls, are exempt if they are used only for that function.

Further information is available from: The Data Protection Registrar, Office of the Data Protection Registrar, Springfield House, Water Lane, Wilmslow, Cheshire SK9 5AX; 0625 535711; or from post offices or your trade association.

USEFUL ADDRESSES

Association of Mail Order Publishers
1 New Burlington Street
London W1X 1FD
071-437 0706

Benn's Direct Marketing Services
PO Box 20
Sovereign Way
Tonbridge
Kent TN9 1RW
0732 362666

The British Direct Marketing Association (BDMA)
Grosvenor Gardens House
Grosvenor Gardens
London SW1W 0BS
071-630 0361/630 7322
The trade body for direct marketing, which includes direct mail.

British List Brokers Association
Springfield House
Princess Street
Bedminster
Bristol BS5 4EF
0272 666900
A professional association of list brokers. The secretary can supply a list of members.

CACI Ltd
Regent House
89 Kingsway
London WC2B 6RH
071-404 0834
Handles ACORN classification of residential neighbourhoods, based on census information. Consumers are classified by the type of residential area in which they live.

CCN Systems Ltd
Talbot House
Talbot Street
Nottingham NG1 5HF
0602 410888
Handles MOSAIC, a targeting
system which offers segmented
geographical areas.

CDMS Ltd
JM Centre
Old Hall Street
Liverpool L70 1AB
051-235 3097
Handles Superprofiles, a geo-
demographic classification
system which can offer 150
different area types.

**Direct Mail Producers
Association (DMPA)**
34 Grand Avenue
London N10 3BP
081-883 7229
Professional association for
agencies only. They can
circulate details of your list
needs to members.

Direct Mail Sales Bureau
14 Floral Street
London WC2E 9RR
071-379 7531
Can put you in touch with
specialist agencies and
suppliers.

**The Direct Mail Services
Standards Board**
26 Eccleston Street
London SW1W 9PY
071-824 8651
Operates a recognition scheme
for direct mail services.

**Direct Marketing Committee of
The Advertising Association**
Mailing Standards Levy
PO Box 744
148-166 Old Street
London EC1V 9HQ

Direct Response Magazine Ltd
4 Market Place
Hereford SG14 1EB
0992 501177
Publishes the *Direct Marketing
Guide,* an annual directory of
services and products.

**European Direct Marketing
Association**
34 rue du governement
provisoire
B-1000 Brussels
010 32 2 2176309
Will provide a list of members
to prospective clients.

Gower Publishing Co Ltd
Gower House
Croft Road
Aldershot
Hampshire GU11 3HR
0252 331551
Publishes the *Direct Mail
Databook,* a directory of
agencies, consultants and
specialist services.

Mail Order Traders Association
25 Castle Street
Liverpool L2 4TD
051-227 4181

Mailing Preference Service
Freepost 22
London W1E 7EZ
Records details of consumers who wish to receive no direct mail shots at all or only that related to their special interests. Names are available to members.

Pinpoint Analysis Ltd
Mercury House
117 Waterloo Road
London SE1 8UL
071-928 1874
Operates the PIN Profiles targeting system which is developed from census information.

Standard Rate and Data Service Inc
3004 Glenview Road
Wilmette
Illinois 60091
USA
0101 312 256 6067
Publish *Direct Mail List, Rates and Data* twice monthly; a complete guide to available US lists.

◀ APPENDIX 3 ▶

FURTHER READING FROM KOGAN PAGE

Commonsense Direct Marketing, Drayton Bird, 2nd edition, 1989

Do It Yourself Advertising, Roy Brewer, 1991

Do Your Own Market Research, Paul N Hague and Peter Jackson, 1987

How to Increase Sales Without Leaving Your Desk, Edmund Tirbutt, 1991

How to Market Books, Alison Baverstock, 1990

Practical Marketing: A Step-by-Step Guide to Effective Planning, David H Bangs, 1990

Running Your Own Mail Order Business, Malcolm Breckman, 1987

Sales Promotion: How to Create and Implement Campaigns That Really Work, Julian Cummins, 1989

Selling to Europe, Roger Bennett, 1991

Successful Marketing for the Small Business, Dave Patten, 2nd edition, 1988

Better Management Skills series

Creative Thinking in Business
Delegating for Results
Effective Employee Participation
Effective Meeting Skills
*Effective Performance Appraisals**
Effective Presentation Skills
*How to Communicate Effectively**
*How to Develop a Positive Attitude**
How to Develop Assertiveness
*How to Motivate People**
Improving Relations at Work
Leadership Skills for Women
Learning to Lead
*Make Every Minute Count**
Managing Disagreement Constructively
Managing Organisational Change
Managing Quality Customer Service
Project Management
Risk Taking
Successful Negotiation
Systematic Problem-Solving and Decision-Making
Team Building

*Also available on cassette.

A full list of books for managers, published by Kogan Page, is available from the publishers at 120 Pentonville Road, London N1 9JN; telephone 071-278 0433; fax 071-837 6348.